Steel Slides and Yellow Walls

Praise for *Steel Slides and Yellow Walls*

"In Alicia Swain's debut poetry collection, a woman's voice calls out of the darkness. With intelligence and precision she speaks—of her own trauma, yes, but also of the earth's, of our society's, of womankind's. Deft with metaphor and lyricism, Swain's poems conjure figures of fierce resolve, speaking against silence with courage. These poems are the sound of a soul pouring forth in order to make and remake a world. A moving first book."

—Colleen Abel, PhD, author of *Remake* and *Deviants*

"'The harbored rage is a necessity.' These six words from Swain's 'Breaking Silence' piece awaiting inside will be one of the many phrases that cling to your brain after reading her latest work, *Steel Slides and Yellow Walls*. It is a liberating, empowering and inspiring read in these dark, uncertain times we face as a society. Swain beautifully and intricately weaves stories of pain, anguish, hope, sacrifice and distrust into her prose, which is as witty and biting as it is heartbreaking and raw. From bodily autonomy to a parent's love to abuse and what it means to be a woman facing the systems built against them in today's world—no stone is left unturned. The brevity in each poem speaks volumes, each stanza strung together effortlessly. She takes you on a journey that ends in freedom, clarity and healing. But not before igniting a fire in you that has burned in her for some time."

—Amy David, journalist featured in *RVA Magazine*, the *Henrico Citizen*, *Midlothian Lifestyle*, GayRVA.com, and OutRVA

"In language both fresh and fierce, Alicia Swain's debut poetry collection *Steel Slides and Yellow Walls* takes the reader on a journey of violent revolution and evolution, a journey toward a young woman's rebirth after years of nearly cracking, nearly drowning. Our guide is a speaker who wrestles, challenges, talks back, and sometimes asks disturbing and ultimately unanswerable questions. These poems offer images of chilling transgressions, ask us to confront uncomfortable memories, witness bodies slammed, bumped, bruised, crushed, and violated.

"Alicia Swain refuses to apply 'lipstick / to beautify the ugliest experiences' (as she writes in '6 AM'). These poems sugarcoat nothing. And yet the collection's final poem, 'Progress,' offers a lovely coda, tells us 'the death / of one purpose can be as beautiful as a birth,' and offers hopeful imagery ('an aroma like red cedar, aged pine / desperate to embark on a new stage of life'). These poems show a writer learning about true love in all its forms, most notably self-love. They leave both speaker and reader moved and restored."

—Alison Condie Jaenicke, teaching professor and assistant director of Creative Writing for Penn State University English Department (Retired)

"Alicia Swain's *Steel Slides and Yellow Walls* is an emotionally powerful book of poetry that is balanced between brutal and beautiful. The evocative language used throughout the book pulls the reader in, making each poem more of a visceral experience than a simple reading. That being said, Swain's perspective is both approachable and accessible through the common language of emotion woven through her writing. We are not just observers of her perspective but are actively thrown into the middle of it."

—Chris Tucker, former educator and contributor to the *Dictionary of Virginia Biography*, a Library of Virginia Project

"Alicia Swain writes of trauma, of violence, but also, of survival and hope. She writes of fathers controlling daughters, of stifling the instinct to grow and learn: *'Fire and brimstone' is a phrase meant for death, / not the stench of pages burning or the razing / of common sense.* The collection builds and the reader must keep going, to see if these girls, these women, survive. We see them saving others and saving themselves: *memories of metal chairs / scraping the church floor, / sunrise a backdrop to strangers / saving lives, often their own.* As Swain presses forward, she reminds us *the harbored rage is a necessity*— and it very much is, for how else do we break free from the constraints that have shackled women for years? She tells us *To be a woman / is to be the very foundation / upon which the world must / build itself* and what a foundation Swain has built."

—Courtney LeBlanc, author of *Her Dark Everything* (2025), *Her Whole Bright Life* (winner of the Jack McCarthy Book Prize, 2023), and others

Steel Slides and Yellow Walls

ALICIA SWAIN

BELLE ISLE BOOKS
www.belleislebooks.com

ISBN (Paperback): 978-1-966369-04-2
Library of Congress Control Number: 2025905575

Designed by Sami Langston
Project managed by Sarah Beam

Published by
Belle Isle Books (an imprint of Brandylane Publishers, Inc.)
5 S. 1st Street
Richmond, Virginia 23219

BELLE ISLE BOOKS
www.belleislebooks.com

belleislebooks.com | brandylanepublishers.com

To every thigh touched by unwelcome hands

Contents

ASK

QUESTIONING MY WAY TO THE GRAVE

They explained to me the importance of asking questions
  often and loudly:

question
  authority
  cruelty
  morality
  god

but when I questioned the roots of it all
  they swaddled me in towels that stunk of mildew
    and suffocated me *quietly.*

Why do they fight for human rights
  through the execution of human life?

Don't question
  life
  peers
  decisions
  fears
  there's no use,

they'll redirect me to the front page of the news and whisper
  that infamy comes only with death
  and never a moment too soon.

I prepare my questions:
  where
  how
  can it end right now

CURRICULUM

How do you expect the children to learn
   what you will not let them understand?
'Fire and brimstone' is a phrase meant for death,
    not the stench of pages burning or the razing
    of common sense.
How do you expect the children to learn
   what you will never allow them to see?

"God didn't build you a world
to hear you disagree."

But centuries of evolution didn't lead you here
   to shutter the thoughts of a transformed species.
How do you expect the children to agree,
   as you cast aside their values
   for an ideology you can't substantiate,
      can't illustrate,
      can't prove
even to beings *so young* they believe flying men
drop gifts in their living room?
You don't expect the children to learn; you strip them
of knowledge because the helm feels miles away,
   because you fear your controlling god
   is losing value in this new world.

Conflict of Interest

If a father were given the opportunity to be judge and jury,
would a child be given the chance to be innocent?
  If a father were given the opportunity to design his children,
  would he desire dominion over daughters?
    If a father were given the opportunity to determine fate,
    would he choose to exist in a world where his child is gay?
      If a father were given the opportunity to save mankind,
      would his selfishness outlive the human race?
        If a father were given the opportunity to take his daughter's pain,
        would his child or self-preservation win?

Anticipation of Conviction

Dependent upon factors beyond our control, we wait
without expectation—but with a sense of consequence.

Where do we stand in the eyes of valuable men and women
so hell-bent on justice, they've lost sight of its meaning?

The hallway smells like oak benches and mahogany tables,
overpriced leather shoes scrape the floor and leave red-hot trails
of blackened tile. Is the rush to grant us our demise or warrant us a fair trial?

These prophecies in our mind may never come to fruition,
but bodies immune to the sharpest end of a sword
never let their heads roll across waxed floors.

Bruised bodies heal too quickly to make a statement in a court of law,
scars join the conversation too late,
                    and so, we wait.

Seen but Not Heard

How many years can a woman spend projecting her voice
to be heard over men? How many years can a woman spend
asking for help to be saved from them?
How many centuries need to pass to grant safety
when the moon wanes and gifts darkness? Bats whisper
in the night and find their way through impassible black depths,
while men crawl through alleyways and risk little more than dollars
in their pocket, an ego at best, as women risk their bodies, their lives,
and know
only un

      r

        e

          s

             t.

A mouse scurries from the hawk flying overhead. How many women
do we need to see dead
before we consider the actions
                  failings
                  wrongdoings
                          of men?

Weight of the World

Tirelessly, I strive to improve what I can control:
bricks laid perfectly flat, stacked
in the palm of my hand—
pounds weighing me down, preparing for defense

one palm open and waiting, staring at the sky,
one palm bearing the weight of the world.

When my mother sang me lullabies,
she never mentioned the need to destroy
everything in my path in order to rebuild.
A child would paint me a villain, a conqueror:
tearing paper from walls,
showing the mess covered
by glue and ornate patterns
created centuries before us.

Do I bury my enemy in rubble and brick,
break down all they've built to recreate it,
or do I graze their temples with clay and concrete
and salvage the cracked foundation beneath?

Skepticism

Despite appearances, validation remains warranted, needed, craved:
without adoration, denial creeps its way between,
whether visible or not, whether intended or not,
when a name falls from cracked lips,
the tone, the volume, each syllable yields dissonance.
Words scratch into stone and leave sweet nothings hardly visible,
and fires burn down tree trunks that celebrated centuries of breath:
where does sanity find its way through skeptical visions, bereft

of passion
of joy
of sanity?

Carve memories and obsession into soft and gentle flesh,
the only way to be certain comforting words won't vanish before death—
is it a task too challenging to expect?

DISQUIETUDE

As the veins in my hands
    rise
    to the surface

and my heart pushes blood
    faster and faster

no kindness or temperament
    could elevate me
        far enough
            to escape this feeling.
Silently
    I weep

as I place one in the barrel
    and spin
    and spin
    and spin

and my heart pushes blood
    slower and slower
        could this be it?

No love could stop my finger
    from holding it down

    only to hear one *click*

and so, still, I weep, alive
    by chance
    by fate
    maybe even
    by God.

EXPERIENCE

At the Party, a Mental Scene

Another night overhearing the sound of aimless babble
while I sit back
seeking not pleasure, but sanity;
my life never cleared of the guilt, my final phrases to a lost life,
such wrathful statements said in youth,

and so, while I sit amongst these fools,
I try to forgive myself for things I cannot undo.
I hold a drink in my hand and feel the beat shake my body so hard
I forget how to breathe,
forget how to see anything in front of me, my mind filled with images
of us holding hands in an open room,
the piano playing the perfect key,
our voices aligned
to sing meaning into words that meant nothing before,

harmony

in its purest form, the only way I should have remembered the sparrow I let slip
through my fingers only days before taking flight.

I hear the beat again,

catch my breath,

listen to the useless ramblings of a drunken man too far gone
to realize he's told the same story
three times
tonight,

about how he kissed a girl
under the stars and moonlight
on a trip to a city he'd never been to before
        but now considered the holiest land
        where he could feel God's divine will

by slipping his tongue down her breasts
while she pressed against the hood of his car.

I listened every time, and the story never changed.
I felt inspired every time, my body craving something
to calm my mind until I, too, forgot my reality.

Door Creaks at Midnight

I asked you not to enter, but the voice of a woman does not rate highly
enough for you to put stock in my choices, you'd rather suppress young voices
      enjoy a violating admittance into a space
with no regard for pain, my brain, for blood, for the sensation of brittle skin
      brushing against a chamber in defense, its walls like wool.
Your embrace was like a bed of nails against my back, each hammered slowly
into my spine,
down my calves, through the soles of my feet. I asked you not to enter,
at least the first time,
but I learned I was better off daydreaming of sand beneath my feet
before walking into the sea and letting the water claim me,
but I learned I was better off laughing at your face than forcing
my fingers into your eyes, but I learned I was better off
pretending to enjoy your drive,
leaving you to fear that you might not be in control anymore.
My door creaked at midnight for weeks, months, years on end,
but now I simply overhear the screaming coming
from much farther down the hall
as she asks you not to enter.

Truce of God

a ceasefire:
when memories stop the waging war from penetrating,
when the bounds of emotional retention give up,
it forces peace with barren tales

images
playing like a slideshow of a stranger's life.

pain existed:
tears barreling down innocent cheeks
too weak to speak loud enough for anyone
to care.

recall:
black suits,
black dress,
black like the television set when the power is cut

recall:
the barbershop, how he stopped
letting the image of his father
stare back at him in the mirror.

a malfunction:
past experiences unable to replay,
moments retained only by the film
leftover on skin in the morning
when there's no way to decipher dreams from reality.

STEEL SLIDES AND YELLOW WALLS

When we sat in the waiting room with its walls
yellow like Fremontia in bloom, I knew
the doctors would come with their white coats,
their stares of judgment as they noticed
the bump on the back of her head.

As I ran my fingers through my hair
in a state of exhaustion, I felt that bump
on my own head, as I felt it once before;
when my body slammed down against
the ruthless floor, the once-private portions
of me bruised and swelled.

And those yellow walls stared down and watched
in a state of silence as I cried, in the same way
she cried when she fell into a pile of rocks
after trying to climb up the metal slide in the heat
of a summer day and bumped her delicate head.

Those yellow walls watched as hands wandered down
the small of my back and punished the parts of me
that only the elite in their white coats
were able to stare at unapologetically.

INFINITY

Half-ton memories crushed my frail skeleton,
and all the avoidance strategies I relied on for years
meant nothing. Half-ton memories pushed my vertebrae down
until I was only a pile of bones and meat,
melding into the ground. An emotionless void,
a mind flush with a tile floor but still aware.
I thought they'd serve me with a garnish: scrape me from the floor
and pour me into the largest pot in the kitchen, boil me
until my consciousness turned to steam,
but that was never the path for me. I woke up
and saw you standing over me in a hospital bed,
my body plastered back together like a living sculpture.
You told the nurse you prayed for my recovery,
and she told you that goes a long way. I guess I needed you
to save me from an avalanche that looked
like a silhouette of your face.

Fulfillment of a Young Girl's Dream

She pondered deeply

the carpet beneath her feet formed static electricity from backing away in socks,
stunned by the rush of air that followed a fist, breezy in its wake

if the induction of a legal binding was worthwhile. There were:

markings on the skin from the sting of a strike against her heart-shaped face—
a lifestyle undesirable, but seemingly impossible to escape. There was:

a dream to be his wife, though marriage seemed a commitment too deep,

but concern had not triumphed soon enough
to beat another night of knuckles
against her soft jawline,

and so, there came an act of faulty love and a change in name.

Six months went by, his name bound to her after she stumbled
in her outfit of contusions
and a paper-white gown, stripped
of every ounce of self-pride and dignity,
light as air.

"That's how we were wed," her shaken voice cried to a fifteen-year-old niece,
                    a child mistakenly falling in love for the first time,
"and this is how I will die," her words somehow darkening a black night.

MELANCHOLY SEA

Your sorrow builds a sea for which no ship exists:
nothing strong enough to float across pensive sorrow,
no oars strong enough to push through tumultuous waves of grief.

You tear down oak and pine, timber from every forest,
rip planks from arks built for God-fearing men who swore
the ocean would swallow the earth and leave no choice
but to float endlessly through time, waiting for a chance to try again.

Your sorrow builds a sea in which no man swims:
no body firm enough to survive the power of the undertow,
nothing prepared for the unpredictable nature that comes with denial
or the moments of clarity that force acceptance.

Bodies wash up on the shore, day after day, and sailboats disappear
into the world beneath their feet because no force could quell your loss.

Manipulate Me

Such a bedside manner you have
as you lower my coffin
       in fact
       I *thank* you
for all you have done as you
hold the pillow and quiet my lungs,
I will not cry—in fact, I thank you for *saving* me,
there's no harm you can cause me
if you free me now, *which is why you won't,*
and I *curse you* for letting my chest ache, my eyes go bloodshot
simply to let me go on knowing
you want nothing more than to dangle my life before my eyes
welled with tears, knowing I can never feel safe—
not to leave nor to stay.

I hear the scrape of stones as you rub them together and light a fire
that engulfs us both, convinces us there's a fiery passion
that nothing can suffocate—
not even you.

AMYGDALA

Reset my olfactory settings.
A window open only a crack
draws aromas of smoke,
freshly cut grass,
all things intertwined
with a memory passed:
deeply embedded
in dimly lit tombs,
catacombs where fingers
reach through walls,
where skulls attempt to stare
with no eyes,

there's cologne
seeping through the cracks,

and with each deep breath,
I smell what my mind
works to forget.
Please reset.
Please reset.
Please

Running Track

Staying in a lane,
within the bounds
pinpricks between
metal gliding
in an attempt to feel
sprinting ahead,
a mind clear
absent
tucking away
unveiling it again
until there's no sign
seeking reprieve
of an endless cycle:
fingertips,
into the skin
nothing
veins p u l s i n g
of worry,
from wonder,
the tourniquet,
and running laps
of where the track began.

CRASHING WAVES

drowning
am   faster   *me* through
I   than I care   *help*   this
         to admit. Please   before   *lost.*
         I am

POLLUTED RIVERS

At the time, speeding down winding roads at ninety-five
felt like a chance to play God.

Fate resting in my hands as I gripped the steering wheel,
      inebriated, yet liberated.

No voice screamed loud enough to alter my decisions,
and if it had, I would have been too numb for consideration.

At the time, a firm belief sat in my chest that I was selfless;
I opted to consider my errors a place to harbor my cruelty,
      my concerns, my rage.

Realistically, such choices opened portals
to the loss of life and the loss of hope. As I leapt out the car door,
I dreamt of deliverance. As I leapt out the car door, a young man
prayed for deliverance from his sins. I took a chance to play God,

as he gripped the steering wheel, seeking aid from a deity. Screaming
loud enough to shake the Earth, and he hoped, Heaven. A firm belief
sat in his chest that he had been selfless, and his end was undeserved;
he was not ready to give way to a loss of life and a loss of hope. Yet, I leapt

I dreamt of deliverance in the form of a painting. A body the ink,
the asphalt a canvas. At ninety-five, my car sped into the waterway
leaving nothing but a speckled rainbow and a broken tree.

Liberate me

24

RECOVER

Day After Day

Fan blades circle, light flashes,

> *yet I stare, endlessly, awaiting change.*

Frames tilt, crooked,

> *yet I stare, endlessly, awaiting change.*

Dust settles on black shelves,

> *yet I stare, endlessly, awaiting change.*

Patience is present for all the mundane, but for myself, I maintain little faith,
yet I stare, endlessly, awaiting change.
My skin shifted from ivory shades to a muted gray,
yet I stare, endlessly, awaiting change.
The crack in the window glass seeps in a cool breeze,
yet I stare, endlessly, awaiting change.
Millipedes shimmy down the cracks in the drywall,
yet I stare, endlessly, awaiting change.
My mind slips from one realm to the next,
yet I stare, endlessly, awaiting change.

SACRILEGE

In my hollow home,
I prayed for hope
and the desecration
of a hardened heart.

> I apologized to her
> for disappearing
> when she needed me
> most.

In my hollow home,
I begged for forgiveness
and the desecration
of self-loathing.

> I apologized to myself
> for disappearing
> when I needed me
> most.

In my hollow home,
I thanked my blood
for not congealing
until my body oozed
with disappointment:

> a gelatinous acid
> sure to air my mistakes
> when I needed reticence.

Trust, an Art Display

as the glass tips, water falls—
droplets sprinkle the page below,
marring an image once clear.
in an attempt to heal, pages tear,
holes form at the surface.

there is no chance of restoration
once left vulnerable, endangered.

before the glass tips, place
the image in a frame, take
the water glass away, bring
safety to a delicate space—
and watch the beauty restore
and pressure fade away.

Melodies in B Major

The key to succeeding is believing
in the power and faith of the music we breathe:
        each note like spores spreading in the lungs,
        branching out from benign nodules
        to the tip of the tongue.
The key to believing is achieving
a sense of compassion for someone besides yourself:
        each body like a needed rest—
        the bars too long
        for belting whole notes
        from the chest.
The key to achieving is retrieving
a sense of purpose in the songs we sing:
        each voice harmonizing like strands of hair
        draping down from follicle to vertebrae
        and gently wrapping around fingertips.

Song of the Sober

somber voices speak
solemn voices ache

an out-of-tune tone
for sorrow's sake

hallways in shadow
simplicity in harm's way

cacophonies of strain
climbing from a barren cave

somber voices disparage
solemn voices disgrace

the birds sing for summer
for only their sake

awake on the patio
far after dark

our paths to survival
never felt farther apart

6 AM

consider the memories lost
as the wind blows arrogance away
like leaves rustling and cracking
along the concrete, a score
similar to frail bones forgotten
in mausoleum walls, crumbling,

the reflection of the sun on teeth,
the laughter pouring from the chest,
all drifting away as defenses fail,
as self-preservation rests, reflect

on memories of metal chairs
scraping the church floor,
sunrise a backdrop to strangers
saving lives, often their own,

lives harboring vacancies
where memories would belong,
if not watered down by suppressants
dancing through veins, lipstick
to beautify the ugliest experiences

Trying to Find Peace of Mind

While you do not bear witness, know I am trying to climb my way out
from this
endless pit
into
radiance.

When you see me drowning, know I will float one day soon;
be patient with my escape from ruin.

This descent led me to depths once undefined,
and maps can't lead me home.

I've fiddled with this token in my pocket for six months now,
but God isn't the one pulling me from the bottom of the sea.

Stones on the Seabed

At the bottom of the ocean, we sit, in tandem,
                    never
                    far
                    apart,
always operating ideally together.
Steady,
        yet steadily moving
                as life shoves us to
                and fro.

        As stable as we seem, we are
                weak independently,
                useless when not a team.
Do we become one, or do we leave ourselves be?

As our surfaces smooth, as our edges feel rounded and clean,
at the bottom of the ocean we sit, in tandem, never far apart
always operating, our actions aligned, though drifting
as life moves us to and fro, seasoned, focused,
stable and growing stronger independently,
the sharpness that bonded us now
distant as a dream,
save for the tug
of sinews
grasping,
waiting,
for us
to join
heart
to
heart.

Omniscient Narrator

With pupils wide, the iris wanders—
completely consumed by a reality
available only within the confines
of a worried, wondrous mind.
A faceless voice reads thoughts
aloud in a tone unprescribed,
perhaps undesired: hesitation
nonexistent in the inner workings.
On the outside, a tired voice stutters
with a lack of confidence, shame,
attempting veracity, but falling short.
Within the mind, ideas feel strengthened,
beyond its boundaries, they feel stifled,
suppressed and suffocating, fighting
for every breath. Never has truth truly fallen

from
these
lips.

SNAKESKIN

I've apologized to you ten times over for who I am:
I left layers of myself strewn across the room with you, and I'm sorry
for every new layer you'll see, no matter how many times you clear my molting,
swear I'm still beautiful, I'll whisper that I'm sorry for what I guilted you to say.

I've apologized to you with every breath I have:
I formed a vibrant layer of skin, a color fitted to what you love, and I'm sorry
for making you feel obligated to appreciate it, no matter how enjoyable it is,
how often you swear it's beautiful, I'll whisper that I'm sorry for what

I've apologized for

           I'm sorry

                 I am who I am.

CONTENDING WITH EMOTION

Intentions aside, provoking realistic perceptions is an impossibility.
Spoken with dignity as the words may be,
silence follows each wish set forth.
Jurisdiction over the mind is left to the nervous system;
disruptions only occur by means of sensation.
Complication arises with intuition.
To feel is to experience the environment in which we exist
with the utmost clarity and purpose; all the same,
to feel is to disrupt the environment in which we exist
and maintain homeostasis. Emotion will disrupt your equilibrium
but do not shut such systems down.

Welcome Signs

When you tap on my door,
do not ask me if you can
come inside. Do not try
to pick the locks. When ready,
you will see the way in
without entering by force.

Do not ask me if you can come
to pick the locks, when ready

tap on my door,
you will see the way in.

MOTHER

Through the storm at midnight, I listen to the gentle tapping of tears
                                                            falling
                                                            from
                                                            heaven,
a coin dances in the palm of my hand,
counting the days since I refrained from apparent sin,
its value meaningless to me now that I know the truth of an overseer,
                                        master of the afterlife
                                        whose tears
                                                wash
                                                        down
                                        my windowpanes.

                                        The only god
                                        watching over
                                        is the woman
                                        who named me.

Oh, How We Have Harmed You

As the sky looks down at me,
I feel the liveliness of the earth
and am consumed by guilt
on behalf of us all for what we
have done. As my feet march
on dampened soil, too far inland
to feel traces of the sea,
I am consumed by guilt,
for what we have done
is beyond repair;
forgive us, love.

Enter Spring

Zephyr, blowing cool springtide winds,
speaks a breathy language only earth
can utter, but all life can comprehend
through the susurration of leaves overhead.
Beauty once blurred in the distance
now beckons seductively, a call to return
to the aspen trees, their yellowish-green leaves
dancing between antlers, a contrast
to fur like an aged penny discarded
by a woman who will never need it to get by.

Flowers Bloom

Apologetic as I seem
graciousness washes over me,

misconstrued conversation guided us here—
my misplaced trust the root of the problem,
the demolition of my trust your gifted solution.

Weeks ago, your eyes failed your stronghold;
your desires became apparent, and thus
       mine diminished.

Presently, sat before you, I ask: *how did we get here?*
But I knew, far sooner than you'll realize
       (if you ever do).

This thankfulness I feel is not unjust.

Many years I've wasted wondering
what it feels like to fire these clay molds
that hold dreams and hopes, each too valuable
to decline myself a chance *to set fire to it all.*

I've wanted this space to grow
       with these tears
and I thank you for:
the soil,
the seeds,
and now,
the sun.

Passivity Ends Here

Venturing from apathy,
     I am lost in a fervid sea
          formed from vulnerability.
               I am invited to find rebirth
                    once I let the water tug me
                         far enough down to feel
                              stones beneath my feet,
                                   salt inside my lungs,
                                       morality at its close,
                    and trust the sea will wash me ashore again.

GROW

Raised as Woman

I'm starting to learn how to grow,
not from soil or grassy fields,
but from piles of stone, rocks
tossed haphazardly across the pavement—
nearly mosaic by design.

I'm beginning to learn how to create,
not from paper, not pen or ink,
but from the iron of blood-tinged streets—
home of the strongest, putrid to the weak,
nearly lethal by design.

I'm starting to learn how to build,
not from brick or wooden boards,
but from burn marks on the skin
carefully placed to conceal betrayal—
nearly beautiful by design.

I'm beginning to learn how to cultivate,
not with open fields or packaged seeds,
but from broken teeth and bundles of hair
piled neatly on the bathroom sink—
nearly nauseating by design.

I'm forgetting to learn of peace,
not by choice or loss of memory,
but from habitual violence done to me,
shoved down with bruising knees—
nearly defenseless by design.

Breaking Silence

don't vilify her for her tenacity

her beliefs are daily incentive
to carry on life purposefully

the harbored rage is a necessity

a woman's words carry weight
when joined with violent grace

men scream on the TV screen

their voices a daily reminder
to carry on in life unrelentingly

their harbored hate is hesitancy

a fear of provocation, even demise
as the quiet ones steadily rise

Private Lessons

Learn many things through failure:
  no excuse can pardon ignorance,
  chaos can unearth truth,
  there is a lot to them that they have not admitted to you.
Learn many things through ignorance:
  it's simple to take advantage of the weak,
  hope can unearth truth,
  there is a lot to them that they will never admit to you.
Learn many things through weakness:
  a strong body means nothing with a soft mind,
  kindness can unearth truth,
  there is a lot to you that they will use to benefit them.
There's no excuse to pardon evil paraded around
  as kindness.
There's no chaos that won't shatter the truth into sharp shards,
  broken glass that fits perfectly between each rib.

COMPLICIT

Complacency makes you guilty:

while you are not the puppet master,
you recognize the problems,
> *the damage done.*

To do nothing, to accept, to ignore, to turn your head—
you're no better than those you say you wish to see dead:
not a drop of purity in your soul greater than your enemy's.

To take a back seat in this world is to grant permission
while the driver runs each person
flat
against
the pavement.

REINVENTION

As I climb the steps to healing,
do not blame me for the pain I've felt
or the way I chose to carry myself—
as my back curled forward, as my legs
dragged from ledge to ledge.
It's taken so long to find my way,
but the path is clear, and now I step,
truth by truth, listen to my armor
tumble down behind me, my helmet
bouncing from landing to landing.
My body no longer knows security,
but the air in my lungs feels freed,
my naked chest knows no limits
but the finite nature of mortality.

Notes to a Younger Self

look up
      nod
            MAKE EYE CONTACT
                                don't use sex as a tool
                                to gauge beauty or worth

laugh at jokes
                put the blades down
                                learn to love yourself
                                instead of seeking love
                                from someone else

don't harbor your parents' anxieties

and forgive yourself for the boy
you said the wrong thing to
before he left this earth
or it will haunt you
forever

                tell the truth about who you are

stop running from artistic passion
                            EMBRACE YOUR YOUTH
                            WHILE YOU'RE STILL YOUNG

What I've Learned from My Parents' Love

When we love, we
do not choose, but
we embrace our chance
to experience, even
once, how sweet
human emotion tastes.
When we love we
enter into a pact, but
we never ask what's right,
we just experience, even
when it feels wrong,
we recover and lick sap
from the tree of life
that we grew
at the foot of our bed.

How She Speaks

Movement is expression:
    the quick *twitch*
        of a disapproving eye,
   the gentle *rise*
      of a guilty smirk.

From aggression manifested in f o o t s t e p s,
                  to a *seductive trot* to the bedroom.

We underestimate the clarity of purpose behind every movement we make.

She curls her toes and her eyes *roll back*
          the moment you caress her thigh,

she shakes her foot *mindlessly*
        when nervousness takes hold.

Her forehead w r i n k l e s as she witnesses
          something she doesn't yet understand.

Communication can be *utter silence,*

    the speed at which she closes her eyes to blink,
    the voice she uses to read, the way her ear wiggles
    while she thinks of all the things she can never undo,
       of all the things she can never forget about you.

EXHIBITION

The artifacts in this museum should be untouchable,
but with a soft brush of the dust, the display of humanity
becomes undeniable. In each brush stroke, there is a child,
a backpack filled with torn-out pages, an adolescent
buried under a blanket of frosty leaves. In each vase,
there is a father with bruised knuckles and empty hands
staring down a barren highway with feet exposed to the brisk
midnight air, tufts of hair blowing away any sense of authority.

Fingerprints darken the corner of the frame, the image
captures a woman standing in tattered clothes at the corner
of Fifth and Main, a cigarette in her left hand and a button
pressed between her right thumb and the tip of her finger.
The sun beats down on her face and reminds the photographer
that natural beauty can't be erased by a bloodied blouse
or jeans worn thin at the knees, that the earth's most precious
creatures are those willing to survive despite their imperfections.

Femininity

To be a woman
    is to be the very foundation
        upon which the world must
            build itself,
            no matter what they take from you
        remember they are nothing,
      not even a single cell,
    without you.

A Body-Focused Mind Withers Away

Now that the closets are shielded by reflective doors, I force myself
to meet my eyes, to cope with the discomfort of peripheral vision—

      my abdomen resting atop barely buttoned jeans,

reminding me of the days
I spent confused about the state of my appearance:
the images of women on the television
striving for perfection,
somehow managing to maintain its facade.
Five meals a day to three to none at all:
sustenance people told me was necessary
had no meaning if the stomach bulged,
if thighs scraped side by side.

Arms shook from frailty, legs struggled to support,
organs fought for life
while suffocated within the tightened confines of my pale, greying skin.

It seemed sensible at the time,
until I pictured a young man fighting in Afghanistan,
and I questioned why I let myself die slowly
while simultaneously worrying about someone fending for his life every day,
listening to the sound of grenades at the back tires of the Jeep
his sergeant howling with excitement at the continuous dodge of death.
I imagined him
wondering every night
if a well-cooked meal would ever again be a luxury,
all while I sat back,
shoving away my homemade dinner,
welcoming death.

As I touch the mirror in front of me, I feel the chill of a lifeless parallel staring back
at my critical eye.

I chuckle and bend down to lace up my boots,
acknowledge,
with no attached emotion,
the roll of skin diving over my barely buttoned jeans,
and I think about the dinner I will make for my lover and I,
who looks at me as though I am the same well-shaped woman I had been
when we met.

Exposure

Miniscule beams of light
t
  r
    i
      c
        k
         l
           e
through the blinds
despite tightly pulled strings
and apparent privacy.
Warmth permeates the room,
stealing every feeling
of inadequacy,
kissing goodbye
to hypothermia
once used as a veil,
a method of defense
so fragile and thin
it never protected
anything at all.

Während Du Schläfst

Occasionally at your side, when I swear to you
that I allow myself to sleep, when we turn off
the lights and invite dreams, I wait,
comprehend
the darkness surrounding us,
watch you sink

into the f r a g m e n t s of your thoughts, the elements of your worries.
Your ideas *scream* in the midst of your snores and tired sighs,
sounds as senseless as those you hear
the first nine months of life,
muttered words hidden
by membrane walls.

Eventually, I stop concentrating on the sounds,
smell the scent of your sleepy breath, released
in flustered huffs. You toss your body
back and forth,
up and down,
seeking a place of comfort.

I nestle my head on the beating in your chest,
and our bodies intertwine to create
a level of warmth reminiscent of the womb
as we fall into an undisturbed slumber.

PROGRESS

The wood grain swirls, and as the log cracks
from the pressure of the axe, its sweet scent
wafts through the air, a reminder that the death
of one purpose can be as beautiful as a birth.
Under the earth, bury the languid and weak,
a body that no longer applies to me, my propensity
for sorrow deceased, my hope for prosperity
released, an aroma like red cedar, aged pine
desperate to embark on a new stage of life.

About the Author

Alicia Swain grew up along Lake Wallenpaupack in Pennsylvania and now resides in Richmond, Virginia, so her poetry is infused with images of both rural and urban life. Her work incorporates feminist themes that aim to highlight the complicated lives of women and members of the queer community. Swain studied English at Penn State University and Eastern Illinois University. Her work has been featured in several online publications, including *The Vehicle* and *Cathexis Northwest Press*.

www.ingramcontent.com/pod-product-compliance
Lightning Source LLC
LaVergne TN
LVHW041203080426
835511LV00006B/727